Born to be Wild
Little Beavers

Christian Marie

Words that appear in the glossary are printed in **boldface** type the first time they occur in the text.

GARETH**STEVENS**

GS

P U B L I S H I N G

A Member of the WRC Media Family of Companies

Never Alone

Baby beavers swim quietly on the surface of the water, closely watched by their mothers and fathers. Only a few hours after they are born, the little beavers, called kits, are able to swim around their family's shelter, or **lodge**. The kits must stay close to their parents because they are still too young to **venture** away from home by themselves. The young kits will follow one of their parents as the adult beavers look for food, cut down trees, and build shelters and **dams**.

Once a year, a mother beaver has a **litter** of usually two to four babies. The kits are born in May or June. At birth, they are already covered with fur, and their eyes are open.

What do you think?

What makes a beaver different from a rat or a **marmot**?

a) A beaver has red eyes.

b) A beaver has a flat, heavy tail.

c) A beaver loves sliding on the snow in winter.

3

A beaver has a flat, heavy tail.

When American beaver kits are born, they weigh between 8 and 24 ounces (227 and 680 grams). The kits drink their mother's milk for only two to six weeks. Then their parents take turns bringing plants for their young to eat.

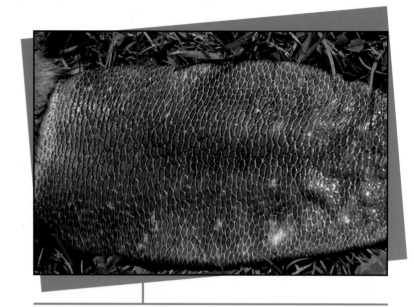

Beavers have large, flat, scaly tails that hold reserves of fat. They use their tails for support when standing on their back legs and for steering and moving forward when swimming.

A beaver has a small head with small eyes, a short nose, and fine whiskers. When the beaver dives underwater, it closes its nose and its round ears.

The strong, compact bodies of beavers are covered with **dense**, waterproof hair that protects the animals from the cold.

Living close to Water and Trees

Beavers build their homes near the shores of rivers, streams, and lakes. Trees such as willows, poplars, and alders grow along the edge of the water. The trees provide food for the beaver family, or **colony**, that lives on the water. The colony also uses the trees to build their lodges and dams. Sometimes, beavers dig canals, or small waterways, across the land, as shortcuts to help them move the trees more easily.

What do you think?

How can you tell that beavers are living on a river?

a) Branches are piled up in the water and trees on the riverbank are cut down.

b) Smoke is coming out of a lodge's chimney.

c) Fences are built along the riverbank.

Beavers spend a lot of time building and taking care of their lodges. Each lodge has two entrances. Both of them are hidden underwater.

Beavers are living on a river if branches are piled up in the water and trees on the riverbank are cut down.

Piles of branches in the water and tree stumps along a riverbank are signs pointing to a beaver's home. The beaver's lodge is built with logs, branches, rocks, and mud. It has two levels. The lower level has entrances into the river. When beavers return home, they stop on this level to shake the water from their fur. The upper level has one room for eating and another for sleeping. Beavers sleep on nests of leaves, grass, moss, and **shredded** wood.

The top of a beaver lodge has a hole, called a vent, through which fresh air enters. During winter, steam comes out of the vent when the inside of the lodge is very warm.

Beavers do not live in the water, but they use water to move and hide the logs and branches they need to build their lodges and dams.

Just before winter, beavers cover their lodges with mud. The mud
helps protect the beavers from the cold when the air temperature
is below freezing.

Lumberjacks and Builders

Timber! A tree falls to the ground. Beavers are nature's **lumberjacks**. Standing on their back legs and using their front teeth, which are powerful **incisors**, beavers are able to slice off pieces of wood from a large tree and bring it crashing down. No tree can stand up against a beaver's sharp teeth, not even the trees with the hardest wood. A beaver leaves a path marked by short, pointed tree stumps.

Working alone, a beaver can cut down a tree more than 4 inches (10 centimeters) in **diameter** in just thirty minutes. Then its family helps the beaver cut the tree into smaller pieces and drag it to the water.

What do you think?

Why do beavers build dams?

a) to have big ponds where they can swim and play with their friends all year

b) to stop their lodges from flooding with water

c) to keep the water around their homes the same **depth**

Beavers build dams to keep the water around their homes the same depth.

A beaver is a great builder, but it does not use tools. It can move any branch it needs using only its teeth. Beavers build remarkable dams out of branches, mud, and trees that they have peeled the bark off of. A beaver's dam backs up the river's water to form a deep pond, so beavers always have enough water near their homes. Their lodges are protected by the water, which prevents other animals from entering.

Most beaver dams are less than 100 feet (30 meters) long, but beavers can build dams up to 1,500 feet (457 m) — the same length as 125 cars parked end to end.

A beaver has a wide space between its front and back teeth. This space helps the beaver hold onto branches when it is moving them.

The sharp edges of a beaver's four incisors are angled, and the **enamel** coating on its teeth is orange.

Beavers build dams downriver from their lodges. The dams are made with piles of branches and are held together with logs, but a river with a strong flow of water can break through it.

Eating Well and Looking Good

After a little beaver stops drinking its mother's milk, it eats only plants, including grass, leaves, branches, and the barks of certain trees. A beaver is able to eat huge amounts of different kinds of plants. The kinds of plants a beaver eats depends on where it lives. Beavers hide and store food underwater in the deep pools that form behind their dams. The water in these pools is too deep to completely freeze, so, in winter, the beavers can swim under the ice to bring the stored food into their lodges.

What do you think?

What does a beaver do besides eat and work?

a) It takes naps in the sun.

b) It takes long baths.

c) It takes trips through the woods with its friends.

A beaver uses its front paws to roll leaves into little balls. When the beaver eats the leaves, the sound it makes is like crumpling paper.

A beaver takes long baths.

Beavers spend a lot of time bathing and carefully grooming their coats. A beaver's coat has two layers. A soft undercoat of fur keeps the beaver warm and an outer layer of long, thick hair keeps the fur dry. The underside of a beaver's body produces an oil that the beaver rubs on its coat to waterproof the outer layer of hair. When beavers swim, their hair lies flat against their bodies, keeping their skin dry. Their coats keep beavers warm, even during freezing cold winters.

A beaver's back paws are **webbed** and act like paddles when the beaver swims. The beaver uses the split claws on its paws to comb the hair on its face and back.

As soon as a beaver is done swimming, it shakes the water from its coat. If its coat stayed wet, the beaver would get cold quickly.

After resting, a beaver grooms its coat. It will
not go back to work without cleaning itself first.

A Close Family

When a male and a female beaver start a family, the two beavers stay together for life. A beaver colony is made up of the mother and father, the youngest kits, and the young beavers born the year before. The mother is the head of a beaver family. She makes the decisions on where to build new dams and when to make the family's lodge bigger. She also makes sure the family works together.

Young beavers live with their parents for about two years. Then, they must leave to find new homes and start families of their own. When they leave their parents, beavers might have to move as much as 30 miles (48 kilometers) or more to find rivers or lakes on which to build their homes.

What do you think?

What does a beaver do when it senses danger?

a) It slaps its tail firmly on the surface of the water.

b) It sprays a bad smell that makes enemies run away.

c) It rounds its back to look bigger.

19

When it senses danger,
a beaver slaps its tail on
the surface of the water.

Beavers have many ways to communicate with each other. They can scream and make noises that other beavers will understand, but, when a wolf gets too close or a bear is nearby, a beaver slaps its tail on the surface of the water. This alarm can be heard up to 1 mile (2 km) away. It helps alert the rest of the family to danger so they can all hide.

When in danger, a beaver will defend itself with its powerful incisors.

After a beaver slaps its tail on the water's surface, it quickly dives underwater. Beavers are very noisy and put on an interesting show when enemies are near.

Bears and wolves are a beaver's main enemies, but hawks, owls, and otters will attack beaver kits. To stay safe, beavers never move too far from the riverbank, where, in case of an emergency, they are always ready to dive into the water.

Beavers are mammals, which means they are warm-blooded and give birth to live babies that drink their mothers' milk. Beavers are also **rodents**. They have two pairs of incisors that never stop growing. Beavers live along rivers and lakes in North America and Europe. American beavers can live about twelve years. They weigh between 25 and 65 pounds (11 and 30 kilograms).

Beavers are related to mice, rats, porcupines, and squirrels.

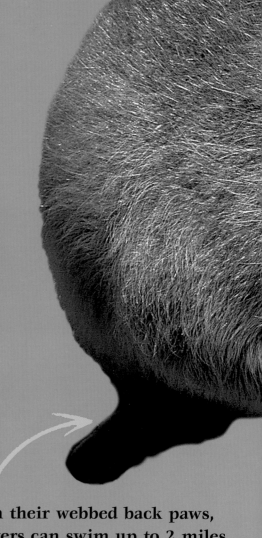

Beavers have long, waterproof coats that are reddish brown or blackish brown.

With their webbed back paws, beavers can swim up to 2 miles (3 km) an hour.

Beavers are the largest rodents in North America. Not including its tail, an adult beaver can be 2 to 3 feet (60 cm to 91 cm) long.

A beaver's tail measures 10 to 20 inches (25 to 50 cm) long.

Beavers have strong claws on the tips of their front paws.

GLOSSARY

colony — a group of the same kind of animal living together

dams — barriers built across rivers or other bodies of water to control the flow of the water

dense — packed closely together

depth — the distance from top to bottom or front to back

diameter — the distance of a straight line that cuts through the middle of a circle

enamel — the hard material on the surfaces of teeth

incisors — sharp front teeth that animals use for cutting food

litter — a group of young animals born at the same time to the same mother

lodge — the home, or den, of a beaver family

lumberjacks — people who cut down trees so the logs can be used for building

marmot — a type of rodent, related to squirrels, which has a fat body, short legs, thick fur, small ears, and lives in a burrow

rodents — animals with large incisors, such as rats and beavers

shredded — cut or torn into tiny strips or pieces

venture — to take on the risks and dangers of an activity

webbed — connected by skin or tissue

Please visit our web site at: **www.garethstevens.com**
For a free color catalog describing Gareth Stevens Publishing's list of high-quality books and multimedia programs, call 1-800-542-2595 (USA) or 1-800-387-3178 (Canada). Gareth Stevens Publishing's fax: (414) 332-3567.

Library of Congress Cataloging-in-Publication Data

Marie, Christian.
  [Petit castor. English]
  Little beavers / Christian Marie. — North American ed.
    p. cm. — (Born to be wild)
  ISBN 0-8368-4734-2 (lib. bdg.)
  1. Beavers—Infancy—Juvenile literature. I. Title. II. Series.
  QL737.R632M2613   2005
  599.37'139—dc22   2004065369

This North American edition first published in 2006 by
Gareth Stevens Publishing
A Member of the WRC Media Family of Companies
330 West Olive Street, Suite 100
Milwaukee, Wisconsin 53212 USA

This U.S. edition copyright © 2006 by Gareth Stevens, Inc.
Original edition copyright © 2000 by Mango Jeunesse.

First published in 2000 as *Le petit castor* by Mango Jeunesse, an imprint of Editions Mango, Paris, France.

Picture Credits (t = top, b = bottom, l = left, r = right)
Bios: C. Thouvenin cover; D. Klees/Fotonatura 15. Colbri: V. and M. Munier 2, 4(b), 16(t); J. P. Paumard 20(t). Jacana: T. Walker 3, 8(b), 13(b); W. Wisniewski 7, 12(b); H. Engels 9; H. Brehm 11; S. Krasehann 13(t); S. Cordier 21; T. Mc Hugh title page, 22–23, back cover. Sunset: Animals 4(t), 5; G. Lacz 8(t); Weststock 10; Hos King 12(t); Animals 16(b), 17, 18, 20(b), 22.

English translation: Muriel Castille
Gareth Stevens editor: Barbara Kiely Miller
Gareth Stevens art direction: Tammy West
Gareth Stevens designer: Jenni Gaylord

Printed in the United States of America

1 2 3 4 5 6 7 8 9 09 08 07 06 05